A New True Book

SOUND EXPERIMENTS

By Ray Broekel

*This "true book" was prepared
under the direction of
Illa Podendorf,
formerly with the Laboratory School,
University of Chicago*

CHILDRENS PRESS, CHICAGO

18705

Marching band

PHOTO CREDITS

Hillstrom Stock Photos—© Ray Hillstrom, 2, 4 (top, bottom right), 7, 8, 10, 13, 19, 31 (2 photos), 41 (2 photos), 42 (bottom), 45 © Anna Photography, 42 (top)

James M. Mejuto—4 (bottom left)

Tony Freeman—Cover, 9 (2 photos), 11, 12, 15, 16, 21 (2 photos), 23, 25, 26, 27, 29, 33, 35, 39

Reinhard Brucker—37 (2 photos)

Cover—Experimenting with different pitches

Library of Congress Cataloging in Publication Data

Broekel, Ray.
    Sound experiments.

    (A New true book)
    Includes index.
    Summary: Briefly discusses sound, pitch, sound travel,
sound waves, vibration, frequency, length, and thickness,
with simple experiments to demonstrate each concept.
    1. Sound—Experiments—Juvenile literature.
[1. Sound—Experiments. 2. Experiments] I. Title.
QC225.5.B74 1983   534   82-17869
ISBN 0-516-01686-5   AACR2

TABLE OF CONTENTS

SOUND

A dog barks.

A cat meows.

A jet plane has its engines running.

What are all these things doing?

They are giving off sound. Those sounds can be heard by people or animals.

DIFFERENT SOUNDS

You can hear many kinds of sound.

Some sounds are high. Others are low.

Some sounds are soft. Others are loud.

Some sounds are scratchy.

What kinds of sounds can you hear right around you?

Make a list of those sounds.

WHAT IS SOUND?

Sound cannot be seen. But sound can be heard.

Sound is made when something vibrates. To vibrate means to move again and again and again.

Some things vibrate up and down.

Some things vibrate from side to side.

There are many sounds in a restaurant.

Or things may vibrate
from front to back.
When something
vibrates, it gives off sound.
Sometimes the vibration
can be seen. Other times
it cannot be seen.

EXPERIMENT

Take a plastic ruler. Lay one end on the edge of a table. Hold that end down with one hand. With the other hand snap the ruler so it goes up and down.

The ruler vibrates. The ruler gives off sound. Try it. (Snap the ruler gently. Don't break it.)

A plastic ruler vibrates and gives off sound.

PITCH

Why are some sounds high and others low?

Sounds have different pitches. Pitch has to do with how fast or slow something vibrates.

The faster something vibrates the higher the pitch.

The slower something vibrates the lower the pitch.

The flute will have a higher pitch than a trombone.

EXPERIMENT

Hold a plastic ruler on the table. Snap the other end.

Listen to the sound.

Now lower the pitch. Move more of the ruler off the table. Hold the ruler down. Snap the other end.

Watch the end vibrate. It does not vibrate as much. The sound will be lower. You have changed the pitch.

Try it.

Now change the pitch so the sound is higher.

Move more of the ruler onto the table. As you hold the table end down, snap the other end.

The end will vibrate more. The sound will be higher because you have changed the pitch.

Experiment with changing pitch.

With more of the ruler on the table the sound will be higher.

SOUND TRAVELS

Sound needs something
in which to travel.

Do you know how sound
gets from the vibrating
ruler to your ears?

Sound travels through
the air. It travels in waves.

EXPERIMENT

You cannot see sound waves. But you can get an idea of how they move.

Fill a washbowl with water. Now touch your fingertip to the top of the water. What happens?

Watch closely. You will see small waves moving away from the place you touched. The waves move outward on the water surface.

Sound waves move away from what is being vibrated in somewhat the same way.

EXPERIMENT

Try this to show air can carry sound waves.

Get a long garden hose. Shake out any water in it.

You hold one end. Have a friend hold the other.

Speak through the hose as if it were a telephone. Have your friend listen. Take turns speaking and listening.

Why can you hear each other? Because there is air in the hose. And sound waves can travel through air.

SOUND WAVES

Suppose a plastic ruler is made to vibrate. When the ruler moves outward, it pushes air away. As it moves backward again, air rushes back into the space. Each time the ruler vibrates a wave is made in the air.

When a person speaks on a phone, sound waves are picked up and sent over the wire.

More waves are made with each vibration. The vibrations are called sound waves.

Sound waves travel in all directions. They cannot be seen. But they can be heard.

EXPERIMENT

You will need a windup alarm clock.

Take the clock outside. Tie a piece of string to the ring loop at the top of the clock. Attach the other end of the string to a clothesline. Let the clock hang about waist high.

Listen for the ticking.

Now lie on the ground underneath the clock. Listen for the ticking.

An experiment with a ticking clock will demonstrate how sound travels in all directions.

Stand in front of the clock.
Stand behind the clock.
Stand at one side.
Stand at the other side.
No matter where you are you will hear the ticking sound.
Sound waves travel in all directions.

AIR, WATER, AND SOLIDS

Sound can travel through air. It can travel through other things, also.

Sound can travel through water. Water carries sound better than air does.

Sound can travel through solids. It can travel through a solid such as wood.

Sound can travel through metal. It travels best through metals.

EXPERIMENT

Compare sounds heard in the air and through water.

You will need two rocks, a friend, and a large glass container. An aquarium will do.

Have your friend strike the two rocks together in the air. Listen for the sound.

Now have your friend strike the two rocks underwater. Put your ear against a side of the container.

Sound travels better through water than it does through air.

The sound that traveled through the water will be louder than the sound made when the rocks were struck in air.

Sound travels better in water than it does in air.

EXPERIMENT

Here's an experiment you can try the next time you are in the bathtub. Let one of the bathtub faucets drip just a little. Listen to the sounds made.

Now put your ears underwater and listen. You can hear the drops hitting the water surface. The sounds will be even louder.

EXPERIMENT

Compare sounds heard in the air and through a solid such as wood. You will need a windup alarm clock and a long stick.

First listen to the clock tick. The ticking sound travels through the air to your ears.

Now put the end of the stick on the clock. Put the other end of the stick to your ear. The ticking sound travels through the wood.

Sound travels through solids, such as wood.

Sound travels through string.

EXPERIMENT

Listen to sound that travels through a solid such as string. You will need a tablespoon, a table, and a piece of string about four feet long.

Tie the spoon at the middle of the string. Loop each end of the string around each of your forefingers. Then place a forefinger in each ear.

Now make the spoon swing so it strikes the edge of the table. You will hear a beautiful sound.

EXPERIMENT

Now listen to sound that travels through metal. You will need a tablespoon, a table, and a piece of very fine wire.

Tie the spoon at the middle of the wire. Loop each end of the wire around each of your forefingers. Then place a forefinger in each ear.

Now swing the spoon so it strikes the edge of the table. You will hear a sound more beautiful than in the last experiment.

Sound travels best through metal.

EXPERIMENT

Compare sounds heard in the air, through a solid such as wood, and through a solid such as metal. You will need a windup alarm clock and a long metal curtain rod.

Put the end of the rod on the clock. Put the other end of the rod to your ear. The ticking sound travels through the rod. You will hear it well.

Compare the sound you hear to that of the ticking coming through the air.

Sound travels through metal better than it does through air or wood.

Compare it to the sound you hear if you hold a long stick to the clock and to your ear.

Sound travels better through metal than it does through air or wood.

PITCH AND FREQUENCY

Pitch depends on how many times something vibrates. The faster a thing vibrates the higher the pitch.

The number of vibrations something makes over a period of time is called frequency. The faster something vibrates the higher the frequency. The slower something vibrates the lower the frequency.

Suppose something vibrates

fifty times in one second.
Another thing vibrates two
hundred times in one
second. Which one will
have the higher frequency?

The second one will. It
vibrates more. So it has a
higher frequency.

FREQUENCY AND LENGTH

How long something is affects the frequency of its vibrations.

Suppose you have two things that are alike except they are of different lengths. Both vibrate for one second.

The short thing vibrates more. It has a higher frequency.

The long thing vibrates less. It has a lower frequency.

EXPERIMENT

You will need three bottles all the same size.

Fill one bottle one third full of water.

Fill the second half full of water.

Fill the third two thirds full.

Air takes up the rest of the space in each of the bottles.

Look at the the lengths of the columns of air. The bottle with the least water has the longest column of air. The bottle with the most water has the shortest column of air.

Suppose you vibrate the column of air in each of the bottles.

Which one will have the highest frequency, or pitch?

Which one will have the lowest frequency, or pitch?

Try this. Blow across the top of each bottle. You will vibrate the column of air in each one.

Which one will have the lowest sound?

The bottle with the longest column of air. It will have the lowest frequency, or pitch.

FREQUENCY
AND THICKNESS

How thick something is affects the frequency of its vibrations.

Suppose you have two things that are alike, except that one is thick and one is thin. Suppose both vibrate for one second.

On a guitar the thicker strings at the bottom of the picture (above) have the lowest pitch.

The thin thing vibrates more. It has a higher frequency, or pitch.

The thick thing vibrates less. It has a lower frequency, or pitch.

37

EXPERIMENT

Get three rubber bands that are of different thicknesses. You will also need a piece of wood, a hammer, and two long nails.

Drive a nail straight into one end of the piece of wood. Drive the other nail straight into the other end.

The nails should be the same distance apart at top and bottom.

Slip the three rubber bands over the nails.

All three bands are stretched the same length because the nails are the same distance apart.

Pluck each band with your finger.

What happens?

The thickest band gives off a sound. It has the lowest frequency, or pitch.

The thinnest band has the highest pitch, or frequency.

The bands give off sound because they are vibrating.

THINGS TO REMEMBER

There are many different kinds of sounds.

Sounds cannot be seen but can be heard.

Sound is made when something vibrates.

Sounds may have different pitches. Faster vibrating things have a higher pitch than slower vibrating things.

Sound travels in waves. It travels in all directions.

City streets have many different sounds.

Something is needed in which sound can travel. Air is one such thing.

Sound also travels through water and solids.

It travels better through water than air.

Sound travels best through metal.

The number of vibrations something makes over a period of time is called frequency.

The faster something vibrates the faster the frequency, or higher the pitch.

The slower the vibrations, the lower the pitch.

The length of something affects frequency.

Two like things may differ in length only. The longer will vibrate slower than the shorter.

Two like things may differ in thickness only.

The thinner will have the
higher frequency, or pitch.

Sound is all around you.

Sound is made when
things vibrate.

Sound is there whether
you hear it or not.

WORDS YOU SHOULD KNOW

air(AYR) — mixture of gases that form the atmosphere of earth

frequency(FREE • kwen • see) — the number of vibrations a thing makes over a given period of time; pitch

pitch(PITCH) — lowness or highness of a sound; frequency

solid(SAHL • id) — something firm that has a more or less definite shape

sound(SOUND) — what is given off when something vibrates

vibrate(VYE • brait) — to make repeated movements up and down, side to side, or front to back

wave(WAIVE) — a regular movement within something when energy, such as sound, travels through it, or on its surface

INDEX

About the Author

Ray Broekel is well known in the publishing field as a teacher, editor, and author of science materials for young people. A full-time freelance writer, Dr. Broekel also writes many other kinds of books for both young people and adults. He has had over 130 published. His first book was published by Childrens Press in 1956. Ray Broekel lives with his wife, Peg, and a dog, Fergus, in Ipswich, Massachusetts.

2023